THE
LUNCH
BUNCH

THE LUNCH BUNCH

TANTALIZINGLY TASTY BROWN BAG IDEAS FOR JUNIOR CHEFS

GINA STEER

CHARTWELL BOOKS, INC.

A Quintet Book

Published by Chartwell Books
A Division of Book Sales Inc.
PO Box 7100
Edison, New Jersey 08818-7100

This edition produced for sale in the
U.S.A., its territories and dependencies
only.

ISBN 0-7858-0387-4

This book was designed and produced by
Quintet Publishing Limited
6 Blundell Street
London N7 9BH

Creative Director: Richard Dewing
Designer: Ian Hunt
Project Editor: Claire Tennant-Scull
Editor: Deborah Taylor
Photographer: David Armstrong
Home Economist: Gina Steer

Typeset in Great Britain by
Central Southern Typesetters, Eastbourne
Manufactured in Singapore by
Eray Scan Pte Ltd
Printed in Singapore by
Star Standard Industries (Pte) Ltd

ACKNOWLEDGMENTS

Special thanks to Spencer and Victoria
Dewing, Tom Lolobo, Gee Hyun Kim,
Nick Seruwagi, James and Lucy Stuart, and
to Bob McNiff of the Burlington Junior
School, Surrey, England.

PUBLISHER'S NOTE

Children should take great care when
cooking. Certain techniques such as
slicing and chopping or using the stove,
oven or broiler can be dangerous, and
extreme care must be exercised at all
times. Adults should always supervise
while children work in the kitchen.

As far as methods and techniques
mentioned in this book are concerned, all
statements, information, and advice given
here are believed to be true and accurate.
However, the author, copyright holder,
nor the publisher can accept any legal
liability for errors or omissions.

Contents

Introduction

If you can read, you can cook, and you're never too young to start. Cooking is fun, and it is a great feeling when you eat something you have cooked yourself. When it tastes good and your family and friends enjoy it as well, then it is really satisfying.

The recipes in this book are easy to follow, with clear step-by-step pictures showing the different techniques required. Some of the photographs are bordered in red, and the instructions are highlighted in **bold text** for safety reasons. You should make sure that there is an adult present, as these steps involve using either sharp knives, hot liquids, or utensils with which you could easily harm yourself.

When cooking, whatever age you are, there are a few basic rules to follow so that you do not hurt yourself or have a disaster in the kitchen. Providing you follow these guidelines, you will find that cooking will give you hours of fun as well as many tasty treats to enjoy.

Read the next few pages first before you start to cook. Then just put on your apron and begin.

Happy Cooking

Before You Begin

▌ One of the most important rules when cooking is to read the recipe right through before you start to do anything. For some recipes, ingredients are soaked overnight or the dish needs to be refrigerated for a long period, and this would be no good if you wanted the dish the same day you started making it.

▌ Check that you have everything you need to make a recipe. Discovering halfway through that you need to pop down to the grocery store to buy one of the ingredients spoils the fun.

▌ When you start to cook, begin with the easy recipes, and once you have mastered these, then move on to those that are a little more complicated.

Hygiene

▌ Hygiene is very important when handling and preparing food, as germs can very easily be passed on through bad habits. Make sure that everything you use is kept as clean as possible, especially your hands.

▌ If you have cuts or sores on your hands, cover them with a clean bandaid.

▌ NEVER use the same chopping boards, knives, etc., to prepare both raw and cooked food; either use clean ones or wash them in between.

▌ Do not play with your pets while cooking and keep them off the work surfaces at all times, especially when food is being prepared.

▌ Make sure that the work surfaces are clean before you start to cook, and always use clean sponges and dishcloths.

▌ Check that all the implements you are going to use are clean before using them. If not, wash them in hot water as often as possible and rinse all the soapy bubbles off. It is better to use rubber gloves to protect your hands so you can use hotter water.

▌ With leftover food or hot food that is to be kept, cool it as quickly as possible, then place it, lightly covered in the refrigerator. Do not leave it sitting out; this is how germs breed and multiply.

▌ Wash all fresh foods such as fruit, vegetables, and salad ingredients before using in the recipe or eating.

▌ Every cook enjoys tasting the food while he or she is cooking, but do not dip and lick; use a clean spoon when you want to taste and wash it after use every time.

First Steps

❙ Put on your apron, tie your hair back, and wash your hands.

❙ Read the recipe through and assemble all the ingredients and implements you need.

❙ Check that it is all right to use the kitchen and that there will be an adult around when you get to the steps that are highlighted.

❙ If, after reading the recipe, you are not sure about a step, ask first so that you understand.

❙ Measure your ingredients accurately.

❙ Try not to make too much mess as this makes cooking harder. Also do not just walk away when you have finished. Clean up afterward, washing up and putting everything away.

Some Cookery Techniques

CHOPPING ONIONS

 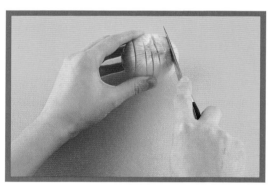 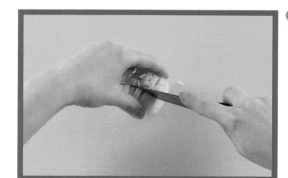

 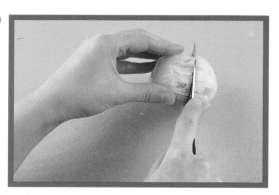 

Peel the onion carefully using a small, sharp knife, but leave the root on. This helps to prevent the juices from making you cry.

1 Hold the onion with one hand, with the root resting on the chopping board. Keep your fingers clear, and cut thin slices from the top almost to the root at the bottom.

2 Turn the onion around in a half circle, then cut again from the top almost to the root.

3 Now place the onion on its side and cut ¼-inch slices.

4 Continue until you get to the root.

GRATING

Place the grater on a chopping board. Peel the vegetable if necessary, then holding the handle of the grater firmly with one hand, rub the vegetable *down* the grater, not up *and* down. Normally, you need to use the side of the grater that has the largest holes. This is known as grating coarsely. Watch your fingers as you get toward the end of the vegetable.

An easy way to grate lemon, orange or lime rind is to use the side of the grater that has the medium-size holes. Rinse and dry the fruit, then hold the grater with one hand and rub the fruit down the side of the grater. By far the best method to remove the rind that sticks on the grater, is to brush it over with a pastry brush.

CHOPPING AND SLICING

Chopping herbs Rinse the herbs and pat dry with paper towels. Cut or break off the stalks, then place the leaves in a cup. Using a pair of scissors, snip the herbs until they are chopped. Use as soon as possible.

Slicing Remember to use a chopping board when slicing or cutting meat, vegetables, etc., and make sure that there is an adult present. It is a good idea to keep a separate chopping board for meat, fish, vegetables, or fruit if you can. If you cannot, then do not forget to wash the board, knife, and your hands in between. Place the food to be cut on a clean chopping board. Then, holding the food firmly with one hand, take a small, sharp knife and cut. Make the cuts away from you and make sure you move away the hand which is holding the food after you have cut a few slices so that you do not end up cutting your hand.

EGGS

Cracking eggs Place a small bowl on the work surface, then crack the egg on the side of the bowl. Gently place your thumbs into the crack in the shell and put your fingers at the top of the egg. Gently pull them apart so that the egg slips into the bowl. Discard the shells.

Separating eggs To separate the yolk from the white, crack the egg, but instead of letting the whole egg slip into the bowl, tilt the egg to one side so that the white can flow into the bowl and the yolk can stay in one side of the split shell. Once the shell is in two halves, put the yolk into the other half of the shell so all the white can flow into the bowl.

Beating Egg whites are often beaten so that air is incorporated into a recipe so that it rises during cooking, or is lighter. Place the egg whites in a clean mixing bowl, making sure that there is no egg yolk with the white (they will not foam if there is any yolk present). Place the bowl on a damp cloth to prevent it from slipping or moving around. With a beater, whip the egg whites until they are white and stiff. A good test is to turn the bowl upside down for a few seconds when you think they are ready. If the whites are stiff, they will not move. Be careful though. Only tip them gently at first. If they move, they are not beaten enough and you need to beat them a bit more.

Creaming Beat butter and sugar together in a mixing bowl using a wooden spoon until the sugar has been completely mixed into the butter. The mixture needs to be light and fluffy.

Whipping Heavy or whipping cream is often whipped before being used. To do this, place the cream in a clean bowl, then place the bowl on a damp cloth and, using a beater, whip the cream until thick. Take care not to overwhip, as the cream will turn to butter.

Cooking Tips

▋ Chicken or turkey is cooked if, when pierced with a skewer in the thickest part of the bird (the thigh), the juices run clear and the flesh is white. If juices or flesh are pink, it needs to cook longer.

▋ Vegetables are cooked if, when pierced with a round-bladed knife or fork, they feel tender to the touch and the implement slides in and out easily. Don't forget however, that most vegetables are better eaten while still slightly crunchy.

▋ Pasta can only really be tested by taste. Carefully remove a piece of pasta and when cool enough, taste it. It should be soft but still retain a bite or chewy texture. This is known as *al dente*.

▋ Pasta is best cooked in plenty of boiling water. It is a good idea to add a few drops of oil as this will prevent the pasta from sticking. As soon as the pasta is cooked, drain thoroughly and use immediately.

▋ Rice is tested in the same way as pasta. It should also feel soft but have a slightly chewy texture or bite. Plain boiled rice is best if rinsed before cooking and then added to double the amount of cold water. Bring to a boil and stir once, then cover the pan, reduce the heat, and simmer for 12–15 minutes or until cooked.

▋ Cakes and cookies are cooked when they have turned golden brown and feel firm to the touch when lightly pressed with a clean finger.

▋ Pastry shells are baked "blind," so make sure that the pastry is cooked properly. To bake blind, either crumple up a sheet of tinfoil and carefully place in the base of the lined pie dish, or, place a sheet of waxed paper in the base and cover it with baking beans. Ceramic baking beans can be purchased and used repeatedly, or you can use dried edible beans which can be used again, but not as often. If the recipe calls for the pastry to be pricked with a fork, do this to make sure that the pastry does not rise during baking.

▋ It is not unusual to find cookery books with both metric and standard units. Always stick to one system as they are not interchangeable. A useful conversion chart for temperatures, weights and measures can be found on page 96.

Storage Tips

It is important that foods are correctly stored so they remain in good condition and safe to eat.

▋ All fresh meat and poultry should be stored on a clean plate, toward the bottom of the refrigerator as soon as possible after buying it.

▋ Fresh fish should also be placed on a clean plate and be loosely covered. Store toward the bottom of the refrigerator and eat within one day of purchase.

▋ All frozen foods should be placed in the freezer as soon as possible after buying.

▋ If you wish to freeze fresh food yourself, first turn the freezer to rapid freeze for at least one hour before you need to use it. Wrap the food to be frozen in freezer wrap or follow the instructions according to the recipe or on the package and place in the fast freeze section. Leave until solid and thoroughly frozen before switching the freezer back to its normal setting.

▋ Fresh green vegetables and salad ingredients should be stored in the crisper of the refrigerator and used, if possible, within two to three days. The longer they are kept, the more their valuable mineral and vitamin content will be lost.

▋ Fresh fruit should be washed before eating and stored in a cool place. Soft fruits should be lightly rinsed and allowed to dry on paper towels just before eating. Do not wash soft fruits and then store them as they will spoil and become mushy.

▋ Potatoes and most root vegetables should be taken out of any plastic wrapping and placed in a brown paper bag and stored in a cool dry place. Carrots will keep in the refrigerator a little longer than other root vegetables, but keep them in a paper bag not plastic, as they could sweat and become wet and slimy.

▋ Eggs should be kept in the refrigerator, as should all dairy products such as butter, milk, and cheese. Cheese is better if stored in a rigid container or box in the refrigerator and wrapped separately.

▋ Bread can be kept in the refrigerator or in a bread box in a cool cupboard. It is always a good idea to wrap the bread to keep it fresher.

Safety in the Kitchen

Heat Use oven gloves or a pot holder when handling anything that is hot. Never try to take something out of a hot oven without using oven gloves.

▐ When using saucepans, hot dishes, or baking trays, use both hands and check first that there is nothing in the way of where you are going to place them once you have removed them from the stove or the oven.

▐ Place hot pans and dishes on a trivet or board. If you feel that a pan or dish is too heavy for you to handle, then ask someone to do it for you.

▐ Keep pan handles on the stove turned away from you. Angle them to the side and not over the burners which, if turned on, will heat the handles, making them too hot to handle.

▐ Do not overfill saucepans as they will then be too heavy to lift. There is also the danger that the contents may boil over if the pan is filled close to the brim.

▐ Call an adult immediately if a fire breaks out. Do NOT try to deal with it yourself.

▐ Do not be tempted to test for heat by placing your hand or fingers on or in anything that may be hot.

▐ Turn off the stove, microwave, and any electrical implements that have been used as soon as you have finished with them.

▐ In addition to informing an adult when you are beginning to cook, you must also tell them when you have finished so they can double-check that electrical implements are safely turned off.

CHAPTER ONE

A Pocket Full of Goodness

Tex-Mex Pitas

SERVES 2 (Makes 4 pita halves)

YOU WILL NEED

2 wholemeal or white pita
   breads
3–4 crisp lettuce leaves, such as
   iceberg
½ small red sweet pepper
1-inch piece cucumber
1 cup cooked chicken
½ cup corn kernels
2 tablespoons tomato and chili
   relish

1 **Preheat the oven to 350°F. Warm the pita bread by placing in the oven for 1–2 minutes. Transfer to a chopping board and, with a sharp knife, cut the pitas in half across the middle.** Open them to form pockets.

2 Rinse the lettuce in cold water and pat dry, then **shred into thin strips** on the board. Place the lettuce inside the pittas, pushing it down to the base.

3 **Carefully take out the seeds and the white membrane from the pepper by cutting out the stalk, then slicing it in two lengthwise.** Rinse and pat dry. **Cut into thin strips.**

   Peel the cucumber and **slice thinly** on the chopping board.

4 Wash the chopping board and knife or use clean ones. Remove any skin from the chicken. Place it on the chopping board and **cut into thin strips.**

5 Holding one pita pocket in your hand, put a few strips of pepper, some cucumber slices and chicken strips on top of the shredded lettuce.

Spoon in a quarter of the corn, then wrap in plastic wrap. Fill the other pita halves with the remaining ingredients, then put two in each brown bag.

6 Spoon a little of the relish into a small container with a lid and add to the brown bag along with two Yankee Doodle Squares (see page 76).

Mini Indian Bites

SERVES 2 (Makes 8)

YOU WILL NEED

8 mini pitas
3 tablespoons mayonnaise
1–2 teaspoons curry powder
½ cup raisins
1 celery stick
3½-ounce can tuna in oil

1 **To warm the pitas, either place them in an oven pre-heated to 350°F for 2–3 minutes or in the toaster for 1–2 minutes. Transfer to a** chopping board, taking care not to burn your fingers and, with a sharp knife, cut a slit in the top of each pita to form pockets.

2 Place the mayonnaise in a bowl and stir in the curry powder. Mix until all the curry powder has been absorbed.

3 Stir the raisins into the curry mayonnaise.

4 **Cut off the top and bottom of the celery,** then rinse under running water. Place on the board and **chop into small pieces.** Stir into the mayonnaise.

5 **Open the can of tuna** and place the contents in a strainer. Stir lightly to drain off the oil, then place the drained tuna in a clean bowl and flake into small pieces with a fork.

6 Stir the tuna into the mayonnaise, then mix all the ingredients lightly together.

7 Spoon the filling into the split pitas.

8 Serve the pitas on a plate garnished with lettuce or wrap in plastic wrap or foil and place in a brown bag.

Tacos with Potato Salad

SERVES 4

YOU WILL NEED

½ pound new potatoes

salt and pepper

2 celery sticks

1 small red apple

juice ½ lemon

½ cup walnuts

1 tablespoon freshly chopped mint

3 tablespoons mayonnaise or
  fromage frais

4 taco shells

2–3 crisp lettuce leaves

2 tablespoons canned refried beans

½ cup Cheddar cheese, grated

1 **Preheat the oven to 350°F.** Scrub or scrape the potatoes and, if large, **cut in half or quarters.** Place in a pan and cover with cold water. Add a pinch of salt. **Place on the burner and bring to a boil, then reduce the heat and cover with a lid. Simmer for 15 minutes or until the potatoes are tender when pierced with a round-bladed knife or fork.**

Remove the pan from the **heat and drain the potatoes through a colander and place in a bowl.**

Trim the celery and wash well, then place on a chopping board and carefully **cut into small pieces.** Add to the cooked, drained potatoes.

2 Wash and dry the apple, **cut into quarters, then remove the core. Chop the apple into small chunks.** Place the lemon juice in a small bowl, then add the apple and turn the apple pieces in the juice until coated. Drain and add to the potatoes.

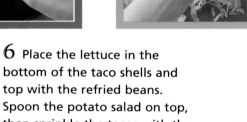

3 **Lightly chop the walnuts in a cup with a pair of scissors** and add to the potatoes with the chopped mint.

4 Add a little salt and pepper, then the mayonnaise or fromage frais. Stir lightly until evenly coated.

5 Place the taco shells upside down on a baking sheet and **warm in the oven for about 2 minutes. Remove and leave to cool before using**.
　Lightly rinse the lettuce in a colander, drain and **shred into thin strips**. Place the refried beans in a small bowl and mash until smooth.

6 Place the lettuce in the bottom of the taco shells and top with the refried beans. Spoon the potato salad on top, then sprinkle the tacos with the grated cheese.

7 Serve on a plate garnished with salad or wrap in plastic wrap or foil and place in a brown bag.

Baby Naans with Winter Salad

SERVES 2 (Makes 4)

YOU WILL NEED

¼ small red cabbage
1 green eating apple
1 tablespoon lemon juice
½ cup corn kernels, canned or
   cooked from frozen
6 radishes, washed
¼ pound ham, sliced
¼ cup walnuts or pecans
3 tablespoons mayonnaise
4 baby naan bread

1 **Place the cabbage on a chopping board and cut off the hard central core and any outside damaged leaves and discard. Using a sharp knife, carefully shred the cabbage into thin strips. Cut out the central white core and discard.**

2 Place the cabbage in a large bowl of water and rinse well. Drain in a colander, then place in a mixing bowl.

3 **Cut the apple into quarters, then cut out and discard the core. Cut into small chunks** and sprinkle with the lemon juice. Add to the cabbage together with the corn kernels. Mix together.

4 **Trim the radishes top and bottom, then chop into small pieces.** Add to the bowl.

5 **Cut the ham into small cubes** and stir into the coleslaw.

6 **Chop the walnuts or pecans in a cup with scissors** and add to the cabbage and mix all the ingredients together.

7 Spoon in the mayonnaise, then mix lightly together with a spoon until all the ingredients are lightly coated.

8 **Split the naan breads with a small sharp knife** and gently open up.

9 Fill the naans with the prepared coleslaw.

10 Wrap in foil or plastic wrap and place in a brown bag, or serve immediately.

Baked Samosas

SERVES 4 (Makes 8)

YOU WILL NEED

1 tablespoon oil
½ small onion, peeled and chopped
1 small celery stick, trimmed
 and chopped
1 tablespoon sweet red pepper, chopped
1 small carrot, peeled and grated
2 teaspoons mild curry powder
¼ pound cooked potato
¼ cup frozen peas, thawed
4 sheets filo pastry
½ stick butter, melted

1 **Preheat the oven to 375°F. Heat the oil in a skillet, then gently saute the onion and celery for 5 minutes or until softened.**

2 Add the sweet red pepper and carrot and continue to saute for 2 more minutes.

3 Sprinkle in the curry powder and cook gently for 3 minutes, stirring all the time. Remove from the heat.

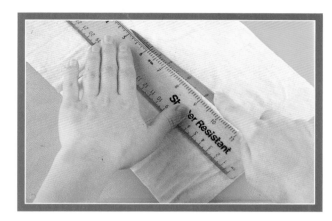

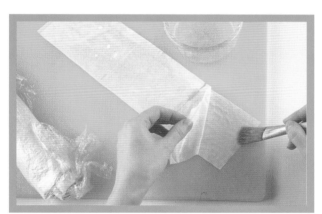

4 **Cut the potato into small cubes** and mix into the skillet with the peas.

5 **Cut the filo pastry in half** to form strips about 3 x 7 inches.

6 Brush one strip with a little melted butter and place a second strip on top. (Keep the remaining filo pastry wrapped in plastic wrap so that it does not become dry and brittle.)

7 Place a spoonful of the filling in the middle of the strip and at the bottom edge. Brush the edges lightly with a little melted butter.

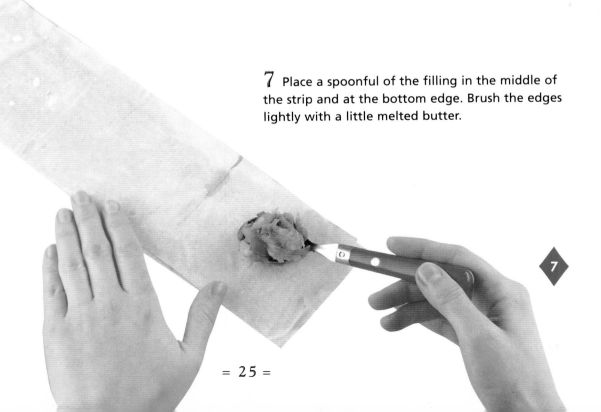

9 Continue to fold the pastry, keeping the triangle shape and folding the stuffed portion away from you until the strip of pastry has been used. Repeat until all the pastry and filling has been used.

10 Brush the pastry with butter before you make the final fold, so that the edges stick together while cooking.

11 Place on a lightly oiled baking sheet, brush with melted butter and **bake for 15 minutes or until crisp.** Cool, then pack into a brown bag or serve hot, warm or cold.

8 Fold the pastry over lengthwise to form a triangle.

CHAPTER TWO

Pick a Stick

Eggplant Satay with Tomato Marinade

SERVES 2–3 (Makes 6)

YOU WILL NEED

FOR THE MARINADE

2 tablespoons tomato paste
2 tablespoons olive oil
4 tablespoons orange juice
1 teaspoon garlic paste
½ teaspoon chili paste

FOR THE SATAYS

1 eggplant
1 tablespoon sesame seeds
6 small wooden skewers

1 For the marinade, in a bowl, mix the tomato paste with the oil, orange juice, garlic and chili paste until well blended and reserve.

2 For the satays, trim the ends off the eggplant and slice thinly lengthwise.

6 **Preheat the broiler to high.** Line the broiler rack with foil and **broil the satays for about 6–8 minutes or until cooked. Turn them occasionally and spoon over a little of the reserved marinade as they cook. Turn down the heat if they start to burn.**

   When cooked, remove the satays from the heat and sprinkle with the sesame seeds. Allow to cool before wrapping, ready to put in a brown bag or serve on a bed of lettuce.

3 **Cut each slice into strips** about ¾ inch wide and place in a shallow dish.

4 Pour the reserved marinade over the eggplant, then turn the strips in the marinade. Cover and refrigerate for at least 1 hour, turning the strips occasionally in the marinade.

   Soak the wooden skewers in cold water for 30 minutes, then drain.

5 Remove the eggplant strips from the dish, allowing the marinade to drain off each one as you take it out, then thread each strip onto the soaked skewers. Reserve the marinade.

Mini Kabobs with Cheese Dip

SERVES 2–4 (Makes 8)

YOU WILL NEED

FOR THE KABOBS

3-inch piece cucumber

4 baby corn

8 cherry tomatoes

¼ pound Edam cheese

8 ready-to-eat prunes (optional)

FOR THE DIP

⅛ pound soft cream cheese

1 tablespoon ketchup

4 scallions, trimmed and finely
  chopped

salt and pepper

8 small wooden skewers or 16
  wooden toothpicks

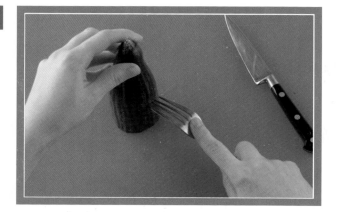

1 For the kabobs, rinse the cucumber and score the skin with the prongs of a fork to give a decorative pattern. **Cut into bite-sized pieces.**
  Cover the baby corn with boiling water, leave for two minutes, then drain. When cool enough to handle, **cut in half** widthwise and reserve.

2 Rinse and pat dry the cherry tomatoes.

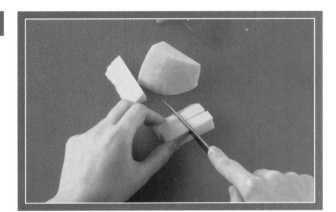

3 Peel off or **cut away the rind from the cheese and discard. Cut the cheese into bite-sized cubes.**

4 Thread the halved baby corn, cucumber, tomatoes, cheese, and prunes (if using) onto wooden sticks. Put on a plate and cover with plastic wrap.

5 For the dip, beat the cream cheese and ketchup together until soft and smooth.

6 Mix in the chopped scallions. Add salt and pepper to taste.

7 Place the dip in small containers and cover; place in a brown bag with the kabobs, or serve on a plate surrounded by the mini kabobs.

Chicken Sticks with Cucumber Dip

SERVES 2–3 (Makes 6)

YOU WILL NEED

FOR THE STICKS

¼ pound boneless chicken breast

2 tablespoons sunflower or olive oil

4 tablespoons freshly squeezed orange juice

1 tablespoon freshly chopped mint

FOR THE DIP

1-inch piece cucumber

1 tablespoon freshly chopped mint

½ cup natural fromage frais or plain yogurt

carrot, celery, and sweet pepper sticks

6 small wooden skewers

1 For the chicken sticks, discard any skin from the chicken and **cut into thin strips** about ¼ x 3 inches. Place in a shallow dish.

2 Mix the oil with the orange juice and mint and spoon over the chicken. Cover and leave in the refrigerator for at least 30 minutes, turning in the marinade occasionally.

Soak the skewers in cold water for 30 minutes.

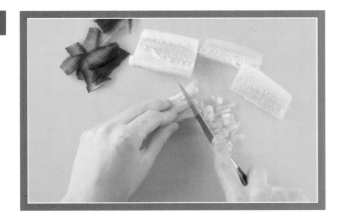

3 For the dip, <u>peel the cucumber and</u> <u>chop into small pieces.</u>

4 Mix the cucumber and mint into the fromage frais or yogurt. Stir well and place into a small serving bowl.

5 <u>**Preheat the broiler**</u> to high and line the rack with foil.
   Remove the chicken strips, allowing the marinade to drain off each one before threading it onto a soaked skewer. Reserve the marinade.

6 <u>**Broil for 8–10 minutes or until**</u> <u>**thoroughly cooked. Turn occasionally and**</u> <u>**brush with the marinade.**</u> Remove from the broiler and serve with the dip and vegetable sticks.

Turkey Satay with Peanut Dip

SERVES 2–3 (Makes 6)

YOU WILL NEED

¼ pound boneless turkey breast
1 red chili pepper
2 tablespoons smooth peanut
   butter
½ cup plain yogurt
juice of 1 lemon (about ¼ cup)
6 small wooden skewers

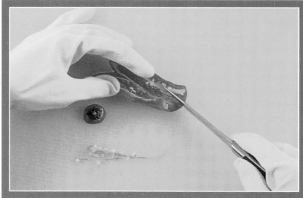

1 Pull off and discard any skin from the turkey and **cut into thin** strips about ¼ x 3 inches. Place in a shallow dish.

2 Using rubber gloves, make a **cut down the length of the chili pepper** and remove the stalk, all the seeds, and the pithy white membrane from the inside. Rinse under cold water, then chop finely. (Take care not to touch your face while handling the chili and wash the rubber gloves and your hands thoroughly afterward.)

3 Place the peanut butter in a small, heavy-based pan with the chopped chili pepper and lemon juice.

4 **Heat gently,** stirring occasionally with a wooden spoon, for about 3–5 minutes or until blended and smooth.

Remove from the heat and slowly stir in the yogurt.

5 Pour half of the mixture over the turkey strips, cover and leave for 30 minutes in the refrigerator. Turn the turkey strips occasionally during this time. Place the rest of the peanut mixture in a small sealable container.

Soak the wooden skewers in cold water for 30 minutes, then drain. Line the broiler rack with foil.

6 **Preheat the broiler to high.** Remove the turkey strips and allow the marinade to drain off each one before threading it onto a soaked skewer. Reserve the marinade.

Broil for 8 minutes or until cooked. Turn occasionally and brush with the marinade.

7 When cool, wrap in tin foil or plastic wrap and pack into a brown bag with the remaining peanut dip.

Salad Stickers

· ·

SERVES 2–4 (Makes 4)

YOU WILL NEED

FOR THE STICKS

4 baby carrots
¼ small sweet red pepper
2 celery sticks
4 scallions
⅛ pound Cheddar cheese
8 cherry tomatoes, rinsed
4 wooden skewers

FOR THE DIP

2 tablespoons mayonnaise
2 tablespoons humus

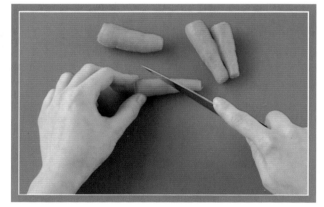

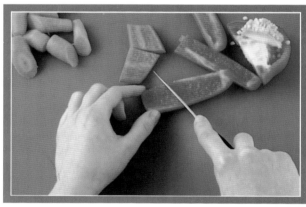

1 For the sticks, scrub the carrots, trim and cut in half if large. **Put in a pan of cold, lightly salted water, bring to a boil, then simmer for 2 minutes, drain and allow to cool.**

2 **De-seed the pepper and discard the pithy membrane, then cut into chunky pieces.**

3 **Trim the celery** and wash under cold water, **then cut into bite-sized pieces.**

4

5

6

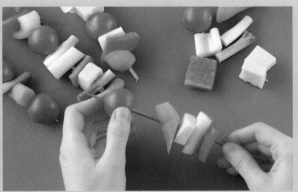

7

4 **Trim the scallions then rinse.
Cut into bite-sized pieces.**

5 **Cut the cheddar cheese into
small cubes.**

6 Rinse the tomatoes
and dry on paper
towels. Thread
all the ingredients onto
small wooden skewers.
Then, either wrap in plastic
wrap and place in a brown
bag or arrange on a plate.

7 For the dip, mix the
mayonnaise with the humus
and place in a small sealable
container and place in the
brown bag, or spoon into a
small bowl and serve with the
sticks.

CHAPTER THREE

Open Toppers

Curried Chicken Wedge

SERVES 4–8 (Makes 8 slices)

YOU WILL NEED

½ pound prepared piecrust

2 tablespoons oil

1 small onion, peeled and chopped

2 garlic cloves, peeled and crushed

1 tablespoon mild curry powder

1½ cups cooked chicken

3 medium-size eggs

½ cup light cream or milk

salt and pepper

1 tablespoon freshly chopped
   cilantro

1 **Preheat the oven to 400°F.** Roll the prepared piecrust out on a lightly floured surface to a circle about 10 inches in diameter.

2 Carefully wrap the piecrust around the rolling pin and unroll it over a loose-bottomed 8-inch fluted tart pan.

3 Gently ease the piecrust into edges and base of the pie plate, taking care not to tear it. Roll the rolling pin over the top to achieve a neat edge. Refrigerate for 30 minutes.

4 Place a sheet of crumpled tin foil or waxed paper and baking beans into the base of the pie shell to stop the piecrust from rising. Bake for 15 minutes. **Remove from the oven and discard the foil or paper and put away the beans.**

5 **Heat the oil in a frying pan then gently cook the onion and garlic for about three minutes or until tender. Sprinkle in the curry powder and cook for two more minutes. Remove from the heat and spoon the mixture over the base of the flan case.**

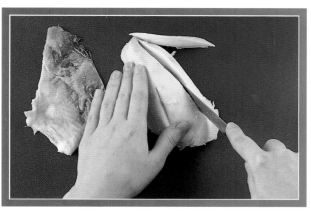

6 Remove any skin or bone from the chicken and **cut into thin strips.** Scatter over the onion mixture.

7 Beat together the eggs, cream or milk, seasoning and cilantro, then pour over the chicken mixture.

8 **Return the pie to the oven** and cook for 15 minutes, **then reduce the oven temperature to 350°F** and continue to cook for a further 20–30 minutes or until set. **Remove from the oven** and cool before cutting into wedges and serving.

Topping Pizza

SERVES 2 (Makes 2)

YOU WILL NEED

1 small bell pepper

3 tomatoes

⅛ pound mushrooms

1 small onion

1 tablespoon oil

2 tablespoons tomato paste

2 individual pizza bases

¾ cup Cheddar or mozzarella cheese, grated

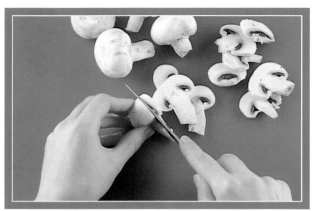

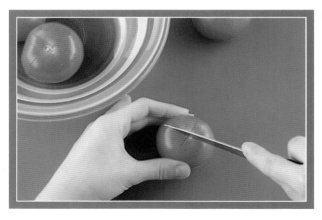

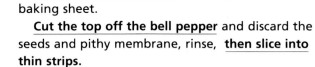

1 **Preheat the oven to 425°F** and lightly oil a baking sheet.

Cut the top off the bell pepper and discard the seeds and pithy membrane, rinse, **then slice into thin strips.**

2 **Make a small cross in the top of the tomatoes, place in a large bowl and carefully cover with boiling water. Leave for 2 minutes, then drain. When cool enough to handle, peel off the skin. Place on a chopping board and chop into small pieces.**

3 Wipe the mushrooms with paper towels and **slice thinly.**

4 **Using a small sharp knife, peel and chop the onion. Heat the oil in a skillet and gently cook the onion for 3 minutes, stirring occasionally.**

5 Add the pepper to the onion and cook for 2 more minutes. **Add the chopped tomatoes and mushrooms and cook for 3 more minutes.**

6 Blend the tomato paste with 2 tablespoons of water and **stir into the skillet, then cook for a further 3 minutes.**

7 Spoon the prepared filling over the pizza bases and sprinkle with the cheese.

8 **Bake in the preheated oven** for 12–15 minutes or until the cheese has melted and is brown and bubbly. **Remove from the oven** and cool completely before wrapping, or serve hot, straight from the oven.

Mini Tuna Tartlets

SERVES 4 (Makes 4)

YOU WILL NEED

⅓ pound prepared piecrust

7-ounce can tuna

3 tablespoons mayonnaise

grated rind of 1 small lemon

2 celery sticks, trimmed and
   finely chopped

5 scallions, trimmed and
   chopped

parsley or cilantro sprigs, to
   garnish

1 **Preheat the oven to 400°F.** Roll the pastry out on a lightly floured surface and use to line four individual pie plates.

2 Prick the bases lightly with a fork and allow to "relax" in the refrigerator for 30 minutes.

3 Place a sheet of crumpled tin foil or waxed paper and baking beans in the bases of the pie plates, then **bake in the oven for 15 minutes. Take out of the oven and remove the tin foil or the paper and beans.** Leave to cool before filling.

4 Drain the tuna, place in a bowl, and flake into small pieces with a fork.

5 Add the mayonnaise to the tuna together with the lemon rind, chopped celery, and 4 of the scallions, and mix the ingredients together.

6 Pile the mixture into the cooked pie shells and sprinkle with the remaining scallion.

7 Either wrap in plastic wrap or foil before placing in the brown bag or served garnished with cilantro or parsley.

Pizza Swirls

· ·

SERVES 3–4 (Makes 6–8 slices)

YOU WILL NEED

FOR THE PIZZA BASE

1 cup self-rising flour
pinch salt
½ teaspoon mustard
   powder
½ stick butter or
   margarine
¾ cup cheddar
   cheese, grated
6–8 tablespoons milk

FOR THE FILLING

2 tablespoons tomato paste
1 small onion, peeled and
   grated
1 sweet red pepper, de-seeded
   and finely chopped
¾ cup ham, finely chopped
1 tablespoon freshly chopped
   parsley
¾ cup cheddar cheese, grated

1 <u>**Preheat the oven to 425°F**</u> and lightly oil a baking sheet.

   For the pizza bases, place the flour, salt and mustard in a sifter and sift into large mixing bowl.

2 <u>**Cut the butter or margarine into small pieces**</u> and add to the flour. With your fingertips, rub the butter or margarine into the flour, until the mixture resembles fine bread crumbs. Stir in the cheese.

   Slowly add the milk and mix to form a soft, but not sticky, dough. Add a little extra milk if necessary. Knead until the dough is smooth and pliable.

3 Roll the dough out on a lightly floured surface to a rectangle of about 8 x 10 inches.

4 For the filling, blend together the tomato paste and 2 tablespoons of water until smooth, then stir in the grated onion, chopped pepper, ham, and chopped parsley.

5 Spread the filling over the dough, leaving a gap of about an inch around the edges. Sprinkle with the grated cheese.

6 Brush the edges lightly with a little water. Roll up from the long end, sealing the filling inside the roll.

7 **Cut into 1½-inch-thick slices** and place on the lightly oiled baking sheet.

8 **Bake in the oven for 12–15 minutes or until golden. Remove from the oven** and cool before wrapping and placing in a brown bag or serving, garnished and arranged on a plate.

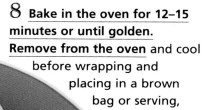

Vegetable Bites

SERVES 4

YOU WILL NEED

FOR THE VEGETABLES

2 celery sticks
½ small cucumber
1 small sweet yellow pepper
1 small sweet red pepper

FOR THE FILLING

4 tablespoons smoked mackerel
   pâté
1 tablespoon plain yogurt
grated rind of ½ a lemon
small bunch of chives
4 wooden skewers (optional)

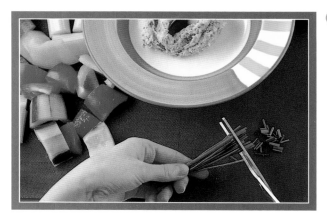

2 **Cut the tops off the peppers** and discard the seeds and white pithy membrane. **Cut into wedges about 1½ inches wide.**

3 Place the smoked mackerel pâté in a bowl, then beat in the yogurt and grated lemon rind. Snip the chives into small pieces and add to the filling. Beat all the ingredients together until smooth and creamy. Spoon the filling into the prepared vegetables. Secure on skewers for ease of carrying if you wish.

1 Trim and rinse the celery and **cut into 2-inch lengths. Cut the cucumber in half lengthwise and scoop out the seeds and discard. Cut the cucumber into 2-inch pieces.**

CHAPTER FOUR

Sandwiches To Go

Burger and Cheese Dinosaurs

SERVES 4 (Makes 1 dinosaur)

YOU WILL NEED

4 hamburger patties
2 teaspoons oil
1 thick French bread
1 tablespoon mayonnaise
  (optional)
few crisp lettuce leaves
4 single cheese slices
2 large tomatoes, sliced
tomato relish or mayonnaise to
  serve

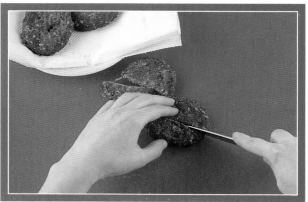

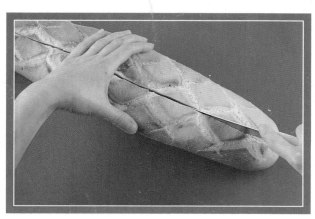

1 **Preheat broiler to high** and line the broiler rack with tinfoil. Place the burgers on the broiler rack. Brush with the oil.

2 **Cook under the broiler for 5–8 minutes, turning at least once, or until cooked.** Drain on paper towels and **cut in half.**

3 **Place the French bread on a chopping board and make a long vertical cut along the top of the loaf.** Carefully open up and spread with mayo if using.

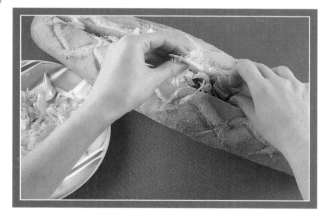

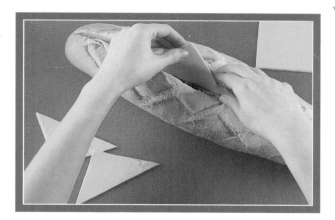

4 Lightly rinse the lettuce and pat dry with paper towels. **Shred the lettuce into thin strips** and place in the base of the loaf.

5 **Cut the cheese slices diagonally in half** and place in the loaf resting on the lettuce, to represent the fins.

6 Arrange the sliced tomatoes and halved burgers in the loaf. Press both sides of the French bread lightly together.

7 **Cut into wedges** and serve with tomato relish or mayonnaise if desired.

BLT

· · · · · · · · · ·

SERVES 1

YOU WILL NEED

2–3 slices bacon

3 slices white or wholewheat bread

2 teaspoons softened butter or margarine

2–3 crisp lettuce leaves, such as iceberg

½ large tomato

1 tablespoon mayonnaise

6 thin slices cucumber

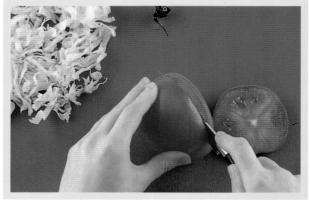

1 **Preheat the broiler to high** and line the broiler rack with foil. **Place the bacon on the rack and cook until crisp, about 5 minutes. Turn at least once** during this time. Drain on paper towels.

2 Spread the butter or margarine on the bread.

3 Rinse the lettuce, pat dry, and place on a chopping board. **Shred into thin strips with a sharp knife.**

4 Slice the tomato thinly.

5

6

7

8

5 Place one slice of bread buttered side up and arrange the cooked bacon on top. Cover with half the shredded lettuce and spoon on a little of the mayonnaise.

6 Top with a second slice of bread, buttered side up, and press down lightly.

7 Cover the bread with the rest of the mayonnaise and arrange the remaining lettuce, sliced tomato, and cucumber on top.

8 Finish with the remaining slice of bread, buttered side down and press lightly together. **Cut in half.**

9 Wrap before placing in a brown bag, or serve immediately.

9

Club

SERVES 1

YOU WILL NEED

3 slices of granary or white bread

2 teaspoons softened butter or margarine, or mayonnaise

1 cup cooked chicken

1 tablespoon cranberry sauce or mayonnaise

2–3 crisp lettuce leaves

1 tomato

½ small onion, peeled

1 Spread the bread with the butter or margarine (or mayo). **Cut the chicken into thin slices.**

2 Place one slice of bread, buttered side up, on a board and arrange the sliced chicken on top.

3 Spread with half the cranberry sauce or mayonnaise.

4 Rinse the lettuce and pat dry. **Shred into thin strips** and place half over the chicken. Cover with a slice of bread buttered side up.

5

6

7

5 **Slice the tomato and onion** and place on top of the bread.

6 Dot with the rest of the cranberry sauce or mayonnaise and cover with the remaining shredded lettuce.

7 Cover with the last slice of bread, buttered side down, and press the sandwich together lightly.

8 **Cut in half** and serve or wrap before placing in a brown bag.

8

Ham and Coleslaw Double Decker

SERVES 1

YOU WILL NEED

3 slices of granary or white bread

2 teaspoons softened butter or margarine or mayonnaise

2 slices of ham

2 teaspoons mango chutney

2 crisp lettuce leaves such as iceberg

2 tablespoons coleslaw

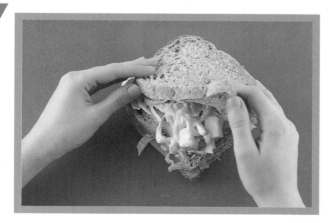

1 Spread the bread with the softened butter or margarine (or mayo) and place one slice on a chopping board, buttered side up. Cover with the ham, then spread with the chutney.

2 Lightly rinse the lettuce and pat dry with paper towels. **Shred the lettuce with a small sharp knife** and place on top of the chutney and cover with a further slice of bread, buttered side up.

3 Place the coleslaw on top of the bread, then cover with the remaining slice of bread, buttered side down. Press together lightly.

4 **Cut in half** and serve with Cheesy Picks (see page 71).

King-Size Bun

SERVES 2

YOU WILL NEED

¼ pound sausage meat

2 scallions

½ small cooking apple

2–3 sprigs fresh mint

salt and pepper

1–2 teaspoons flour

2 buns

2 crisp lettuce leaves, shredded

2 teaspoons mango chutney

2 canned pineapple rings,
   drained

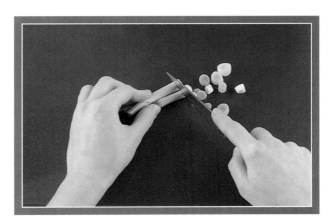

1 **Preheat the oven to 400°F.** Place the sausage meat in a bowl and break it up with a fork.

2 **Cut off and discard the root and most of the green part from the scallions and chop finely.** Add to the sausage meat in the bowl.

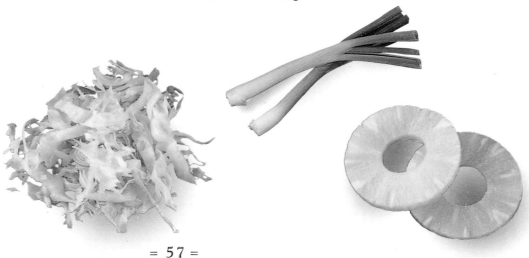

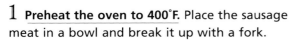

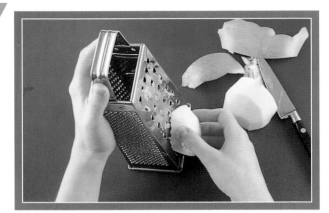

3 **Core the apple and peel, if preferred. Grate on the coarse side of the grater and add to the sausage meat.**

4 Place the mint in a cup and **chop with a pair of kitchen scissors.** Add to the bowl and season the mixture with salt and pepper.

5 Mix the ingredients together with clean hands, then form into two round burger shapes.

6 Coat with the flour, place on a baking sheet, and **bake in the oven for 15–20 minutes or until cooked and lightly golden in color. Remove from the oven.**

7 **Split the buns** (you can lightly toast the buns if you wish) and cover the bases with the lettuce.

8 Place the sausage meat burgers on top. Dot with the mango chutney.

9 Top with the pineapple ring, then cover with the top of the bun.

10 Wrap when cool to place in a brown bag or serve immediately while still warm.

CHAPTER FIVE

Mouthwatering Salads

Rice as Nice

SERVES 4–6

YOU WILL NEED

FOR THE SALAD

½ cup long-grain rice
½ cup frozen corn
½ cup frozen peas
8-ounce can red kidney
   beans or mixed beans
1 cup cherry tomatoes

FOR THE DRESSING

3 tablespoons olive oil
1 tablespoon lemon juice
1 teaspoon sugar
a pinch of mustard powder
1 tablespoon freshly
   chopped cilantro
salt and pepper

1 For the salad, place the rice
in a saucepan and cover with
cold, lightly salted water. **Bring
to a boil, then reduce the heat
and simmer** for 12–15 minutes
or until the rice is tender but
not soft.

2 **Drain the rice in a colander**
and place in a large mixing
bowl.

3 **Cook the corn and peas together in a pan of gently boiling water** for 3–5 minutes, or until tender.

4 **Drain** and add to the rice.

5 Pour the can of red kidney beans or mixed beans into a colander and rinse under cold running water. Add to the rice and mix lightly.

6 **Rinse the tomatoes and cut them in half**, then add to the rice and mix again until all the ingredients are evenly distributed.

7 For the dressing, place all the remaining ingredients in a screw-top jar and shake vigorously until they are well blended.

8 Pour onto the rice salad and toss lightly.

9 Serve immediately or cover and store for up to 8 hours in the refrigerator.

Chicken and Pasta Salad

SERVES 4–6

YOU WILL NEED

½ pound boneless chicken breasts

2 tablespoons hoisin sauce

4 tablespoons orange juice

¼ pound dried pasta shapes

1 teaspoon sunflower oil

¾ cup seedless green grapes

1 cup cherry tomatoes

4 scallions

3-inch piece cucumber

2 tablespoons olive oil

salt and pepper

1 tablespoon freshly chopped cilantro

 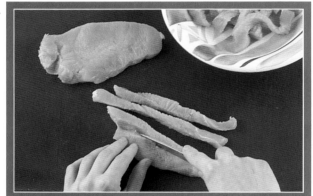

1 Discard any skin from the chicken and **cut into thin strips**, place in a shallow dish. In a pan, **warm the hoisin sauce,** then mix with half the orange juice. Pour over the chicken, cover, and leave in the refrigerator for 30 minutes. Spoon the marinade over the chicken occasionally during this time.

2 **Bring a medium-sized pan of salted water to a boil and add a little drop of oil. Cook the pasta for 8–10 minutes or until cooked. Drain and place in a bowl.**

3 Drain the chicken, discarding the marinade, and **heat the remaining oil in a skillet. Stir-fry the chicken for 5–6 minutes. Remove from the skillet with a slotted spoon and add to the cooked pasta.**

4 Wipe or rinse the grapes and tomatoes. If large, **cut the tomatoes in half**, then add to the bowl.

5 **Trim the scallions by cutting off the root, and some of the tough green tops and removing any rough outer skin. Place on a chopping board and chop,** then add to the pasta and chicken mixture.

6 **Wash, or peel the cucumber if preferred, then chop it into small pieces.** Add to the bowl and mix all the salad ingredients lightly together.

7 Mix the remaining orange juice, olive oil, salt and pepper, and the chopped cilantro together and pour over the salad.

8 Toss lightly together, then place in a container. Serve immediately or cover and store in the refrigerator for up to 1 day.

Sputniks and Beans

SERVES 3–4 (Makes 8 sputniks)

YOU WILL NEED

½ pound ground lamb
1 small onion
1 tablespoon pine kernels,
  chopped
grated rind ½ lemon
1 cup fresh white bread
  crumbs
1 tablespoon freshly
  chopped mint
salt and pepper

1 egg yolk
¼ cup blanched almonds
8-ounce can red kidney beans
½ small sweet red pepper
4 scallions
1 celery stick
2 tomatoes
2–3 tablespoons ketchup

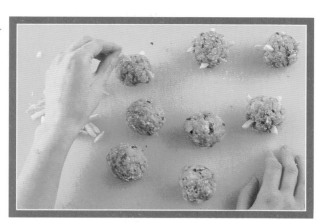

1 <u>**Preheat the oven to 375°F.**</u> Place the ground lamb in a mixing bowl and break up the lumps with a fork.

2 <u>**Peel the onion, leaving the root on, and grate on the coarse side of the grater.**</u> Add to the lamb with the pine kernels, grated lemon rind, bread crumbs, chopped mint, and salt and pepper to taste.

3 Stir the ingredients together, then add the egg yolk and mix thoroughly with your hands.

Shape the mixture into small balls and place in a small, lightly oiled baking pan. <u>**Cut the almonds into two or three to make short "sticks"**</u> and use to stud the meatballs. Cook in the oven for 15–20 minutes or until cooked.

4 **Remove from the oven** and drain on paper towels.

5 Drain and rinse the beans in a colander or strainer and place in a small mixing bowl.

6 **De-seed and chop the sweet pepper into small pieces. Trim off the root and the tough green part from the scallions, removing any tough outer skins, and chop finely.** Add to the beans.

7 **Trim the celery and chop into small pieces. Chop the tomatoes,** then add them with the scallions to the beans along with the ketchup.

8 Mix together and serve with the meatball sputniks.

Turk's Veil

· ·

SERVES 4–6

YOU WILL NEED

FOR THE SALAD

¼ pound couscous
½ cup frozen mixed
  vegetables
1 tablespoon freshly
  chopped mint
1 tablespoon freshly
  chopped parsley
⅓ cup raisins
1 cup baby button
  mushrooms

FOR THE DRESSING

4 tablespoons olive oil
2 tablespoons orange juice
a pinch of dry mustard
  powder
1 teaspoon clear honey
1 teaspoon ground
  cinnamon
salt and pepper

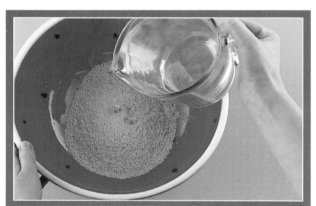

1 For the salad, place the couscous in a large bowl and **cover with boiling water.** Cover with a clean dishcloth and leave to stand for 5 minutes or until all the water has been absorbed.

2 Spoon the couscous into a strainer and **place on top of a pan of gently simmering water.** The bottom of the strainer should not touch the water.

3 **Steam for about 5–8 minutes, forking the couscous occasionally to separate the grains. Remove from the heat and place in a bowl.**

4 **Bring a fresh pan of lightly salted water to a boil and add the frozen vegetables. Bring back to a boil and cook for 3–5 minutes.**

5 **Drain and add to the cooked couscous.** Add the chopped herbs with the raisins and mix all the ingredients lightly together.

6 Wipe the mushrooms with paper towels, then **slice**. Add to the couscous.

7 For the dressing, place all the remaining ingredients in a screw-top jar and shake vigorously until well blended.

8 Pour the dressing over the couscous, toss lightly, and serve.

Crunchy Bites

Cheesy Picks

MAKES about 40

YOU WILL NEED

½ cup all-purpose flour
½ teaspoon mustard powder
a pinch of cayenne pepper
½ stick butter or margarine
⅛ pound mature Cheddar
cheese
1 tablespoon sesame seeds

1 **Preheat the oven to 400°F**
and lightly oil a baking sheet.
Sift the flour, mustard powder,
and cayenne pepper into a
mixing bowl.

2 Add the butter or margarine
to the flour.

3 Using your fingertips, rub in
the fat until the mixture
resembles fine bread crumbs.

4 <u>**Grate the cheese using the rough side of the grater**</u>, then stir into the flour and butter or margarine mixture.

5 Using your hands, mix to form a smooth but not sticky dough, adding about 1 teaspoon of cold water to help bring the mixture together.

6 Knead lightly until smooth, then roll out on a lightly floured surface to form a rectangle about ¼ inch thick.

7 Cut into thin strips about ¼ x 3 inches. Place on the baking sheet.

9

8 Lightly brush with a little water and sprinkle with the sesame seeds. **Bake in the oven for 12–15 minutes or until golden brown.**

9 Allow to cool before removing from the baking sheet. Arrange on a plate and serve, or store in an airtight container for up to 3 days.

Oaty Chews

MAKES 8 slices

YOU WILL NEED

1 stick softened butter or
   margarine
¼ cup golden sugar
3 tablespoons corn syrup
¾ cup oats
½ cup chocolate chips

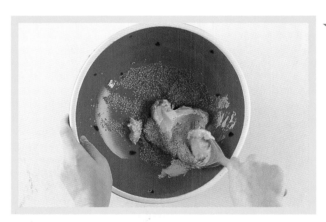

1 **Preheat the oven to 400°F**
and lightly oil a square baking
pan.

2 Cream the butter or
margarine and sugar together
until pale and soft.

3 Brush a tablespoon with a
little oil, then use it to measure
out the corn syrup. The oil will
keep the syrup from sticking to
the spoon. **Warm the syrup in a
small saucepan,** then add to the
creamed mixture and beat in.

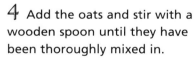

4 Add the oats and stir with a wooden spoon until they have been thoroughly mixed in.

5 Stir the chocolate cooking chips into the mixture.

6 Place the mixture in the prepared pan and smooth the top with a palette knife. **Bake in the oven for 20 minutes or until pale golden.**

7 **Remove from the oven and, using a round-bladed knife, mark into bars.** Leave in the pan until completely cold.

8 Serve on a plate, or store in a container for up to a week.

Yankee Doodle Squares

MAKES 9 squares

YOU WILL NEED

¾ cup all-purpose flour

1 stick softened butter or margarine

¼ cup superfine sugar

3 tablespoons smooth peanut butter

¼ pound cooking chocolate

 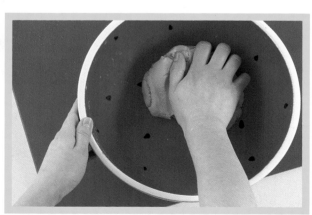

1 **Preheat the oven to 350°F** and lightly oil a square baking pan.

Sift the flour into a mixing bowl, then add the butter or margarine.

2 Rub in the butter or margarine using your fingertips, until the mixture resembles fine bread crumbs. Stir in the sugar.

3 With your hands, knead the mixture until it comes together and forms a ball in the center of the bowl.

4 Place in the pan and gently pat out the mixture until it fills the base of the pan and is an even thickness.

5 Prick the surface with a fork, then **bake in the oven for 20 minutes or until pale golden**.

6 **Remove from the oven** and,using a round-bladed knife, gently spread the cooked cake with the peanut butter, making sure that it is evenly coated.

7 **Break the chocolate into small pieces and place in the top of a double boiler over gently simmering water. Stir until melted.**

8 **Pour the melted chocolate over the peanut butter.**

9 Spread with a knife until the top is completely covered.

10 Allow the chocolate to set before cutting into squares.

11 Serve or store in an airtight container for up to a week.

CHAPTER SEVEN

Sweet Delights

Chocolate Crackles

MAKES 8

YOU WILL NEED
¼ pound cooking chocolate
½ stick butter or margarine
3 tablespoons corn syrup
2 cups cornflakes
½ cup chopped almonds

1 Break the chocolate into small pieces and place in a large, heavy-based saucepan.

2 Add the butter or margarine to the pan.

3 Brush a tablespoon with a little oil, then use it to measure the corn syrup. It will then easily run off the spoon into the pan.
Place the saucepan over a gentle heat and cook gently, stirring occasionally with a wooden spoon until the ingredients have melted.

4 **Remove from the heat** and stir until the mixture is smooth.

5 Add the cornflakes and nuts and stir with a wooden spoon until they are well coated in the chocolate mixture.

6 Spoon the cornflake crackles into small paper cases.

7 Leave until set before serving. Store in an airtight container.

Chocolate Fudge Delights

MAKES 8 triangles

YOU WILL NEED

¼ pound bittersweet cooking
  chocolate
1 stick butter or margarine
¾ cup soft brown sugar
1 cup self-rising flour
2 eggs
a few drops of vanilla extract
½ cup flaked almonds
½ cup glacé cherries
1 tablespoon sifted powdered
  sugar

1 **Preheat the oven to 350°F** and lightly oil a square baking pan. Break the chocolate into small pieces and **place in a pan over a low heat.**

2 **Add the butter or margarine and melt slowly over a gentle heat.** Stir occasionally with a wooden spoon until smooth and free from lumps.

3 **Add the sugar and stir well until thoroughly mixed.**

4 **Remove from the heat. Sift the flour into the pan and stir in.**

5 Break the eggs into a bowl and beat. Add to the pan and stir in.

6 Stir in the vanilla extract and flaked almonds.

7 **Chop the cherries on a chopping board,** then rinse in warm water and pat dry with paper towels.

8 Stir in the cherries, then **spoon the mixture into the prepared pan. Bake in the oven for 30 minutes, or until cooked and a skewer inserted into the center comes out clean.**

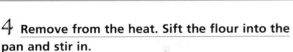

9 **Remove from the oven** and mark into four squares.

10 Cut each square in half to form triangles.

11 Leave until cold before removing from the pan and dust with powdered sugar.

Apple Crunch

SERVES 2

YOU WILL NEED

1 pound cooking apples
1 teaspoon ground cinnamon
⅛ cup light soft brown sugar or
   to taste
grated rind ½ lemon
½ stick butter
½ cup fresh white bread crumbs
¼ cup almonds, chopped
Mint sprigs, to decorate

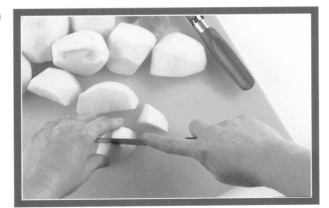

1 **Peel the apples and discard the cores. Cut into chunks** and place in a pan with 2 tablespoons of water.

2 **Place the pan over a moderate heat and cook, stirring occasionally, for 10–12 minutes or until the apples are soft and cooked.**

3 **Remove from the heat** and cool slightly before pouring into a food processor. **Blend to form a purée,** then spoon into a small mixing bowl.

4 Stir in the cinnamon, sugar, and lemon rind and mix lightly together. Cool and reserve.

5 **Melt the butter in a skillet, then sprinkle in the bread crumbs. Cook over a gentle heat, stirring frequently for about 5–8 minutes or until the bread crumbs become crisp and golden.**

6 **Stir in the chopped almonds, then remove from the heat.**

7 Layer the apple purée and bread crumbs in small dishes, ending with bread crumbs. Serve lukewarm or cold, decorated with a sprig of mint.

8 Cover the tops before packing into a brown bag.

Fruity Sticks

SERVES 4–5 (Makes about 20)

YOU WILL NEED
2 ounces seedless green grapes
2 ounces seedless red grapes
½ small melon
2 satsumas

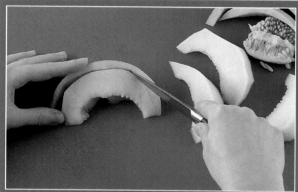

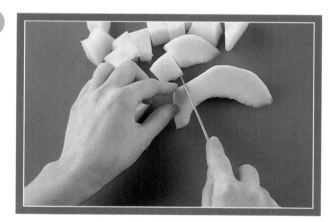

1 Take the grapes off their stalks, then rinse in cold water and pat dry with paper towels.

2 Discard the seeds from the melon and **cut off the skin.**

3 **Cut the melon** into small bite sized pieces.

4

5

4 Peel the satsumas and take off as much of the white pith as possible.

5 Thread alternate pieces of fruit on to cocktail sticks.

6 Serve on a plate or wrap in clear wrap and place in a lunch box with a small tub of fruit-flavoured fromage frais to use as a dip.

6

Ready Jello Go

SERVES 3–4

YOU WILL NEED

1 pack raspberry-flavored gelatin
1 pack lime-flavored gelatin
1 pack orange-flavored gelatin

1

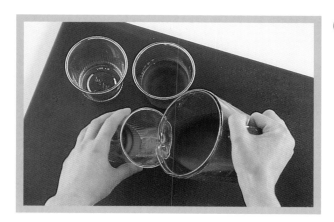

2

1 Place each gelatin in a separate jug or bowl and **pour over each one ½ cup of boiling water.** Stir until the powder has dissolved, then add 1¼ cup of cold water to each one.

2 Pour a layer of raspberry gelatin into 3–4 clear plastic dishes, place in the refrigerator, and leave until set. (If you want to have them set at an angle, when you put the first layer in to set, prop the dishes at an angle, making sure that the gelatin does not tip over while setting. Repeat with the second and third layers.)

3 Cover the first layer of raspberry gelatin with a layer of lime, and again place in the refrigerator until set.

4 Finally pour the orange gelatin into the dishes and leave in the refrigerator to set.

5 Serve or cover the tops and pack in a brown bag with a small spoon.

Smoothies

· ·

SERVES 3–4

YOU WILL NEED

¼ pound dark cooking chocolate

1¼ pints milk

2 tablespoons cornstarch

1 tablespoon sugar

2 teaspoons grated chocolate or fresh sliced strawberries, to decorate

1 Break the chocolate into small pieces and put in the top of a double boiler. Measure 4 tablespoons of milk into a separate jug and reserve. **Add the rest of the milk to the pan with the chocolate.**

2 **Simmer over gentle heat and allow the chocolate to melt, stirring occasionally.**

3 In a small bowl blend the cornstarch to a smooth paste with the reserved 4 tablespoons of milk.

4 **Bring the chocolate milk to a boil, then pour in the blended cornstarch.**
   Reduce the heat and stir until the mixture thickens. Cook for 1 minute, still stirring.

5 **Remove from the heat** and stir in the sugar.

6 Pour the mixture into small containers. Cool slightly before placing in the refrigerator for at least 4 hours, or until set.

7 Decorate with either a little grated chocolate or sliced strawberries.

Strawberry Mousse

SERVES 3

YOU WILL NEED

½ pound ripe strawberries
1 teaspoon gelatin
2 tablespoons orange juice
½ cup Greek-style yogurt
1 teaspoon sugar or to taste
3 strawberries, to decorate

1 Rinse the strawberries and pat dry on paper towels.

2 **Place in a food processor and blend to form a purée.** Pass the strawberry purée through a fine strainer, to remove the seeds. Place in a bowl.

3 Place the gelatin in the top of a double boiler with the orange juice and **place it over gently simmering water. Heat gently, stirring occasionally with a wooden spoon until the gelatin has dissolved. Cool slightly.**